Journal of

the
backyard
kids

Baseball edition

<u>Dedication</u>

To the backyard moms and dads who raised us,
The backyard husbands who supported us,
And the backyard kids who were the inspiration for this book.
Keep chasing your dreams and never stop being #BackyardKids
(no matter how old you get)

_____

1

This book is property of the Somerville Bulldog

Baseball team. If you do not play for the Bulldogs,

DO NOT OPEN this book. If found, please return to

215 Bulldog Road in Somerville.

Are you seriously still reading?! The last page clearly

said,

DO NOT OPEN

But here you are.

This means one of three things:

1. You do not like listening

2. You are a FAKE Somerville Bulldog OR

3. You are a baseball fan who is in for an EPIC story

Which one is it? I'm guessing number 1 and 3. Who

doesn't love a little combo?

Now that you're here, I guess I need to explain. Inside this journal, you will find great memories from an amazing baseball team inside the city of Somerville.

We weren't always **AMAZING.**

In fact, last season our team was awful (awful like the Brussel sprouts your parents make you eat!!!)

We didn't just have a losing record.

We lost EVERY. SINGLE. GAME. We were miserable.

Crying after each game like:
- Cats with onions in their eyes
- A kid whose birthday party got cancelled
- A baby with a diaper full of poop

This is Coach Rodriguez. The meanest coach in the history of sports. He was so mad at our losing record last season, he broke his phone over his left knee. Snapped it like a little twig.

He has no clue we call him Rod, so don't spill it, ok?!

Then, Coach Rod banished phones from all the land. He was desperate for a win, no matter the cost. Phones went missing. Obsolete. Never ever to be seen again. Like the baseball that got eaten by the BIG bad wolf.

But for real, he banned phones for the entire team. Before, during, and after games - even at practices. NO electronics. We HATED Coach Rod for this. He totally crossed a line!

 We told our parents in hopes they would

organize some revolt, but nope, nothing.

Not one of them. Zilch.

Fast forward to this season. NOTHING CHANGED.

No phones. No technology. The rule followed us. It was

like the world's most embarrassing season was

happening **all over again...** This meant one thing.

We needed a plan, FAST!

We weren't going to let Coach Rod have

the final say – that is what brings

you here.

Inside this journal you will find top secret letters, game

recaps, and drawings passed to and from players of the

Somerville Bulldog Baseball team.

Usually, the player of the

game (announced by

Coach Q) is the one who

writes the recap.

A recap is a fun way for a player

to share their likes and dislikes. They also get to share

the highs and lows of the game.

Look at that smile!! Can't you tell Coach Q is the man? His son Jayden plays on our team too!

As for me, my name

is Kolt- Kolten Ryan.

You can call me,

"Kolt the Bolt."

I thought of the idea to start this journal. A way to

keep our conversations going even if we couldn't use

phones. Don't be fooled by the word JOURNAL. It's not a

diary where we confess our deepest darkest secrets.

Or is it?

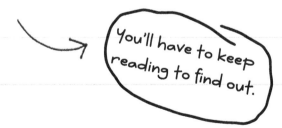

You'll have to keep
reading to find out.

So, sit back, relax.

Grab a Somerville favorite, sunflower seeds.

And hold onto your caps.

WE ARE GOING FOR A RIDE

ONE WAY TO PLAYOFFS

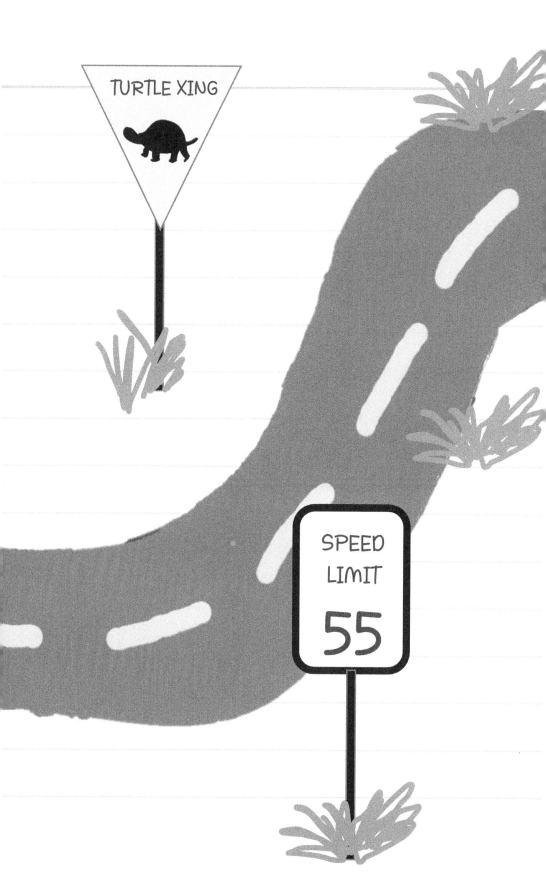

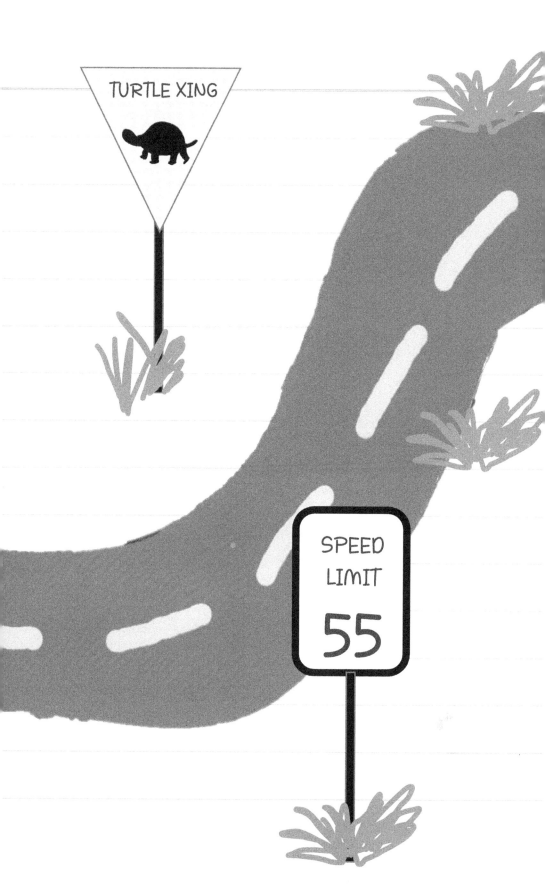

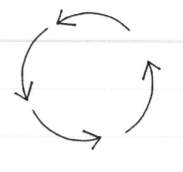

Entry One
-try outs-

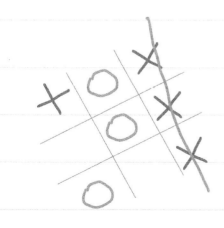

My pal, Spence, spotted it first. He quickly turned to

me with a smile and shouted,

"The second-best day of the

year is here, man.

"Let's goooo!"

There it was - the posting

for Somerville Bulldogs

Baseball tryouts.

Saturday, March 1st. The day we

had all been waiting for.

Me and Spence -
the kid who
whooped me in tic -
tac - toe on the
last page.

After the awful season last year, you can imagine how we felt seeing that flyer. It felt like 10,000 butterflies flapping away in our bellies! Nervous because of the smelly pits of last season, but excited to show off our new skills and get this season going.

The days on the calendar moved like snails, but tryouts finally came...

...and in the blink of an eye, they were over.

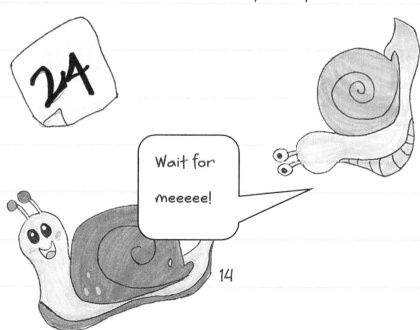

Wait for meeeee!

14

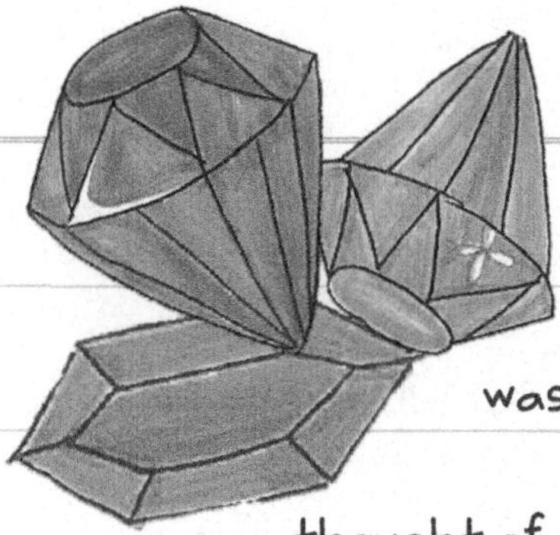

Waiting to hear who made the team

was not easy. My best friend, Jack,

thought of a gem of an idea - but it was going

to be risky...

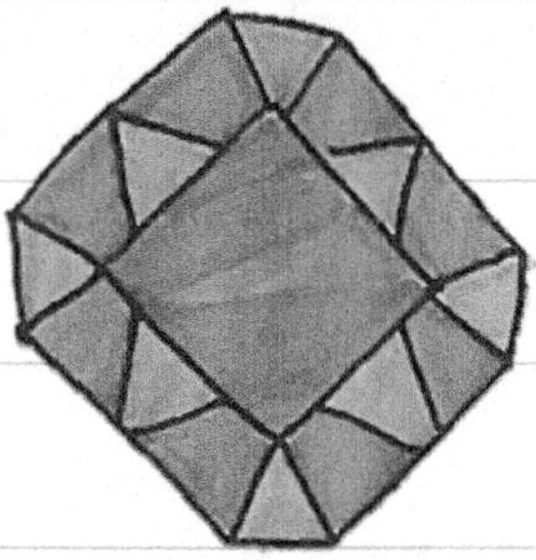

Selfie of me
and Jack

15

... Do you love a thrill? You know, the feeling

of your heart beating out of your chest?

If you do, follow the trail to the 'X' to find out

what Jack had planned.

I double dog dare you to flip the page...

you made it this far.

COMMENCE
Operation Spy Game

'Operation Spy Game' is a dangerous undercover mission run by Somerville's finest baseball players.

What is the purpose of 'Operation Spy Game'? To spy on the coaches during their top-secret meeting where they talk about tryouts and get a glimpse at who will make the team.

What we learned during the operation is as follows:

- The coaches sit around a table and eat wings (are they chicken wings or the wings of some other mythical creature, we can't be sure)

- Coaches drink green slime

- They also talk about something called taxes (I am pretty sure that has nothing to do with baseball)

We also learned that Quinn (the kid you see in the bottom right corner) likes to trash pick. He found something clutch at the bottom of a trashcan smelling of onions, fish, and farts (the only part of his body we could see were his feet sticking out – he was that deep in garbage).

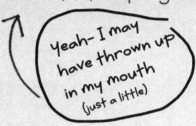

Yeah– I may have thrown up in my mouth (just a little)

Quinn did NOT uncover a list of kids who made the team – however, it wasn't a total loss! We still found out an awesome piece of information...

Shhhh – it's me. QUINN!!!

Ugh- not the Kingston Knights. They are really good, they creamed us last season. Partly because they cheated...

Somerville Bulldogs Schedule

Home vs. Fish Street Sharks

Home vs. Kingston Knights

Away vs. Briardale Bandits

Away vs. Slyville Foxes

Away vs. South Philly Blazers

Home vs. Blue Rockets

Away vs. Green Devils

Home vs. Pickleville Cucumbers

19

This measly piece of paper smelled worse than a

MILLION dads eating a bowl full of baked beans...

And you know what they say about beans, right?

In case you don't, let me introduce you to **the one**, and

only one, poem that will be included in this journal.

Ode to a bean

    Beans, beans, they're good for your heart.

The more you eat, the more you FART.

    The more you FART, the better you feel.

So eat beans for every meal. (author unknown)

Don't let me get distracted by fart talk, I need to keep

this moving so we can get to the good stuff...

(LIKE WHO MADE THE TEAM!)

FAST FORWARD

A couple of days after our undercover operation –

Spence turned to me during our walk to school and

whispered, "Kolt. Don't totally freak. Stay cool. I think

I see the posting right there on that tree." As we got

closer he shouted, "Yea boy, there it is. Kolt this is it!!"

It was the official team list.

Somerville Bulldogs Travel Baseball Team

1. Amir Youseff (2nd base)

2. Jack James (right field)

3. Nash Walker (short stop)

4. Spence Bryan (3rd base)

5. Caleb Smith (left field)

6. Jayden Bell (center field)

7. Kolten Ryan (pitcher)

8. Brendan Banks (1st base)

9. Ace Werley (catcher)

10. Parker Reeves (back up pitcher, 3rd base)

11. Henry Koin (1st, 2nd and/or short stop)

Oh no, where's Quinn's name?

The list had shockers.

Some of the same players from last year made the

team. Others weren't so lucky. A few new guys were

added who bring great experience.

New or not to the team, the coaches didn't miss a

beat. Practices picked back up with our new,

improved team and the **no phones rule continued.**

With all the changes happening, there was so

much to say. Without texting or electronics, our

letters to one another were non-stop.

Before we get to the letters, let me

introduce you to the kids of Somerville...

SOMERVILLE

Amir Youseff

"Here to hit dingers and make you laugh"

Spence Bryan

"Numbers are my favorite"

Parker Reeves

"Doing big things"

Caleb Smith

"I don't smile"

Kolten Ryan

"Your go-to pitcher"

BASEBALL

Nash Walker

"The guy blowing the bubble, he's my go-to"

Brendan Banks

"Nash 'The Smash' is the man"

Jayden Bell

"Ball all day"

Henry Koin

"I didn't do it"

Jack James

"Trying to become a millionaire by age 12"

Ace Werley

"Fastest feet in town"

April

Sunday	Monday	Tuesday	Wednesday	Thursday	Friday	Saturday
					1	2
3	4	5	6	7	8	9 Bowling at 6:00
10	11	12	13	14	15	16
17	18 SPRING TRAINING	19	20	21	22	23
24	25	26	27	28	29	30

May

Sunday	Monday	Tuesday	Wednesday	Thursday	Friday	Saturday
1	2	3	4	5	6	7
8	9	10	11	12	13 End of spring training	14
15	16	17 Practice at 4:30	18	19	20	21 Morning practice
22	23	24	25	26 Practice at 4:30	27	28
29	30					

Entry Two
-spring training-

||||| ||

READER BEWARE

Some of the kids on the team cannot write neatly. Most of us never even wrote a letter before this journal came along. I don't do much in the writing department (outside of homework!).

But, when you want to talk to your friends, and have no way to text, you'll do the unthinkable. We went old-school.

(almost as far back as when dinosaurs roamed the Earth)

Dear Coach Rodriguez and Coach Q.

My name isn't on the list, that's ok. I just started practicing this year. But I really love baseball.

I wuz wondering if I could come watch the team practice this season? Pick up some pointers to come back stronger next year.

From, Quinn Reed

Hello Quinn,

Be at practice on time!! This does <u>not</u> mean you' re on the team, but you can watch. See you at Spring Training.

-Coach Rodriguez

Yo Jayden,

Did you see Quinn's name missing from the roster? I feel so bad, he is ALWAYs practicing. It's not that he isn't good, he just needs to learn more about the game. Let's have him practice with us on our off days. What do you say?

From, Spence

PS - I don't think I've ever written a note before. It's not as good as sending a text, but it's not *that* AWFUL (don't tell Coach Rod)

Hey Spence,

Stinks about Quinn, but he can tag along with our crew.

And make sure u watch out for Caleb. He's always trying to work your stat book to help him look better (don't forget what he did last year!!)

Sidenote: Kolt (if you are reading this) — what are you using to get the letters to stick? I had to use my gum to get this sucker in here. It's why this page is so sticky. Sorry!

Catch ya later-

Jayden

Jayden, it's called tape!

But enough of the letters for now, let's pass the book to Parker and have him talk about Spring Training since Coach Q just announced him as player of the preseason!

From, Kolt

PLAYER of
spring training

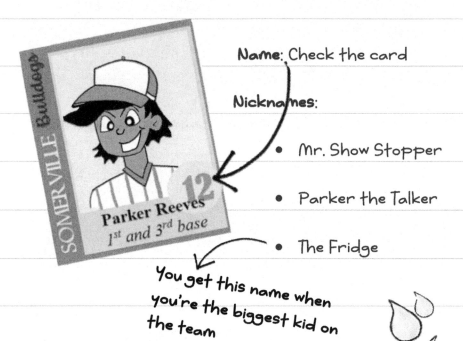

SOMERVILLE Bulldogs

Parker Reeves
1st and 3rd base

12

Name: Check the card

Nicknames:

- Mr. Show Stopper

- Parker the Talker

- The Fridge

You get this name when you're the biggest kid on the team

I love all things: TV, cheese fries (like super cheesy,

drippy HOT deliciousness), WWE, and cannon balls (the

bigger the splash THE BETTER!) BUT I absolutely HATE:

Chores (stop making me clean, mom!) and Mondays (the

official worst day of the week!)

Recap:

spring training

May 18

Alright, alright! It's Parker here with the first official entry of this journal! We look like a totally different team compared to last year. Maybe the no phones rule does have us more focused.

I have been a BEAST during spring training so far. All over the diamond, making defensive plays. Running, sweating. LOTS of running and sweating.

WE ARE A TEAM ON A MISSION!!! A mission to be little league champs and nothing will distract us from that!

However, there is something distracting us a little bit.

The sneaky, cheating Kingston Knights.

See, we caught the Knights creeping around our

practices and SPYING. Camera phones taping us and

stealing pitching signs. The Knights were in disguise,

talking into walkie talkies and all.

I'm guessing word got out about

how much better we have

been looking and it has our

rivals shaking in their cleats.

The Knights live ten minutes away. Rumor has it, even our parents' grandparents were rivals with them when they were kids!

Too bad for the Knights, a real observant player

noticed they were coming around during our

Wednesday night practices and watching from

the train tracks (the tracks sit way behind

our first baseline).

NO ONE is going to spy on us and get away with

it! Especially not after how much we have

dedicated to becoming a better

and stronger team!

PAY BACK IS COMING

But in order to get payback,

I need to reach out to my man, Amir.

He is the best prankster!!

May 19

SPECIAL REQUEST FOR AMIR-
I want to get revenge the next time
the Kingston Knights spy on our
practice (and you know there WILL
be a next time).

Can you devise the most epic
PRANK EVER for when they strike
again?! No one messes with the
Bulldogs!!

From, Parker

Yo Parker,

This has me so pumped! I have
been waiting to try this prank I saw
on TV! It involves balloons filled with
green paint. Let's just say the
Kingston Knights will NEVER forget
our team color.

Your go - to guy for all things
mischief,

Amir

We have been at the fields for about two weeks

since my request to Amir and no one has

spotted you know who.

Trust me, when we

finally catch the Knights,

you are going to witness the

most epic prank of all time.

"Amir's Paint Balloon Palooza" will be

in full effect!

... It's just a matter of time!

Hopefully before Opening Day!!

You know what else is just a matter of time?!

Catching Coach Rod with something in that

crazy mustache of his....

Breaking news!!!

EXTRA, EXTRA

READ ALL ABOUT IT!

Issue #1

Stop what you are doing, put everything down.

We interrupt this journal recap for a

BREAKING MUSTACHE REPORT

The following is based on mysteries discovered in Coach Rod's hairy mustache. Much to gruesome to keep to ourselves.

The items found are foul, creepy, and sometimes unbelievable. Everything you read is completely true and not exaggerated at all.

Have your barf bag ready.
We will not be held liable for vomit clean up.
You've been warned.

BREAKING MUSTACHE REPORT

Issue #1

We interrupt this recap with critical news!

Coach Rod had the BIGGEST, green, *slimy,* booger stuck to his crazy, bushy mustache!

A booger so big it looked alive! A booger so big it put last year's broccoli stalks to shame!

How does he NOT feel it occupying space on his face? It's one of the greatest mysteries of the world! That along with Babe Ruth's eleven-time homerun record in the majors (can you say legend?)

Will he top this week's mystery mustache? Or will Coach Rod look in the mirror and realize what is happening?

Until then, we cannot stop laughing!

Somerville Game Schedule

Home vs. Fish Street Sharks (June 1)

Home vs. Kingston Knights (June 9)

Away vs. Briardale Bandits (June 15)

Away vs. Slyville Foxes (June 22)

Home vs. Blue Rockets (June 29)

Away vs. South Philly Blazers (July 6)

Away vs. Green Devils (July 13)

Home vs. Pickleville Cucumbers (July 20)

Playoffs (teams to be determined)

Entry Three
-opening day-

PLAYER OF THE GAME

Name: Jack 'The Snack'

Position: Right field

Saying "Money can't buy happiness, but it can buy ice cream and ice cream makes people happy."

LIKES

- snacks (of course) and selling them for profit
- buttered noodles (with SALT)
- basketball
- video games

disLIKES

- being grounded
- running laps
- when people don't pay their snack bill
- school
- cleaning

recap:

vs. Fish Street Sharks

June 1

I can't believe I got player of the game! Thanks Coach Q- you are the man! Our first game verse the sharks was on opening day... the best day ever. Well, one of the best days besides:

- My birthday

- SUMMER

- Christmas

It started out pretty rocky. We were a man down because someone had a case of the tummy troubles.

Minutes before the game, Ace started dancing around like there were ants in his pants. He would have been lucky if it was just that - but it was a tummy full of vomit. He said the nerves were getting to him. He puked EVERYWHERE.

Not having Ace in the lineup was HARD! You see, the problem was we weren't playing like a team. It's almost like Ace's tummy troubles and nerves were contagious! We couldn't get out of our head. Every at-bat ended in strikeouts. We couldn't make any plays in the field either. Which meant only one thing. We needed to...

Rise up!!!!

To rise up means that you don't back down when facing hard times.

You continue to push yourself and your team.

It's a Coach Q thing. He brought it up last year

when we were stuck in our slump.

You never stop RISING UP to the challenge

We all started chanting RISE UP. Over and over.

Jumping up and down. Getting super pumped -

like no other.

"Rise up, Rise up, Rise up..."

And then, we had CHILLS. The kind of chills when your hair stands straight up on your arm and your body gets shaky.

It was just what we needed to get this game moving! (Well, all of us except Caleb. He is the team grouch and nothing makes him smile.)

We morphed into a new team! After some great at-bats that loaded the bases, Jayden iced the cake with a HUGE GRAAAANNNDDDDDDDDDDD SLLLAMMMMMMMMMMMMMMM

Meet Caleb. The kid who never smiles. Rumor has it he has never laughed. IN HIS LIFE.

Lucky for us, we made fish sticks out of

those guppies. Starting off the season

undefeated!!! Can you believe it?!

Have you ever had a fish stick before? They sound gross, but they are crispy, CRUNCHY, fried sticks that are oh so good… I wouldn't expect a pretty fish like this to be so flavorful… BUT THEY SURE ARE!!

Now that the first win is under our belts...

time for me to focus on my main priority:

my snack shack business.

From the Desk of:
"Jack the Snack"

I am the PROUD owner of

Jack "The Snacks"

dugout business.

I am your guy for ... snacks, bubble gum, baseball cards and beyond.

You name it, I can get it!

As long as you pay your bill, we are good!

TO FUTURE CUSTOMERS:

On the *next* page, tape all your food requests for the season, I will deliver by 3pm the next day!

Jack's Special Request Orders

ORDER NUMBER   PLAYER NAME

3   Parker

Jack- my mom wont give me my allowance this week (didn't clean my room, it wasn't THAT dirty). Just some old bowls on the floor that were growing some type of black stuff on the sides.

Mind if you start a little bill that I can pay off next time my allowance comes in?

Youre the man snacks!!

Jack's Special Request Orders

ORDER NUMBER   PLAYER NAME

02

YOO JACKIE SNACKIE- FOR NEXT GAME I NEED:

- 11 NERD ROPES
- 103 BUBBLE GUMS
- XL BLUE ENERGY SODA POP
- 10 SEEDS (NOT FOR ME)

TY!!

AMIR

NEED.
MORE.
BUBBLE.
GUM.

FROM. AMIR

Jack's S
ORDER NUMBER

3

50

Hot dog $1.00
Peanuts $0.50
French fries $3.00
Popcorn $1.00
Bubble gum $0.25
Pretzel $2.00
Popsicle $1.00
Salt.....TOTALLY FREE.

Hands down best ice cream around — Mini Melts Ice Cream. Crazy good and fun to eat!

Somerville Game Schedule

✓ Home vs. Fish Street Sharks (June 1) (4 – 2 us)

Home vs. Kingston Knights (June 9)

Away vs. Briardale Bandits (June 15)

Away vs. Slyville Foxes (June 22)

Home vs. Blue Rockets (June 29)

Away vs. South Philly Blazers (July 6)

Away vs. Green Devils (July 13)

Home vs. Pickleville Cucumbers (July 20)

Playoffs (teams to be determined)

53

Entry Four
-kings~~t~~ Knights-

Not these guys...
anyone but the
Kingston Knights

PLAYER OF THE GAME

SOMERVILLE Bulldogs

66

Caleb Smith
left field

Name: not writing in this book

Likes: not writing in this book

Dislikes

- Writing in this stupid book
- Almost all people
- Losing
- The sun
- Smiling

Don't look for any likes — There aren't any!

55

recap:

vs. KINGSTON KNIGHTS

June 9

Let's keep this simple.

What were you thinking of – making me player

of the game?

In a game we LOST!

No.

Absolutely not.

Not writing a recap.

Bye.

June 10

Hey Caleb, it's your boy Reeves. I was shocked you didn't write anything else in the book... I can help...

I get why you're so mad! Losing to the Knights brings on flashbacks from last season. Just thinking about it makes my skin crawl, my mouth water, my eyes bleed.

There is a reason they are our biggest rivals...

Last season the score was back and forth the entire game because SHOCKINGLY the Knights were choking and so were we (it was one of the hottest days of the year and the skin was melting off my body!)

It looked like the same game this time too! Back and forth, back and forth like a game of ping-pong!

But then...

OMG- OMG- OMG

Wait, I don't have time to finish the recap for Caleb.

Coach Rod just SENT A TEXT to the parents (yes, you read that right - a text!!) ...

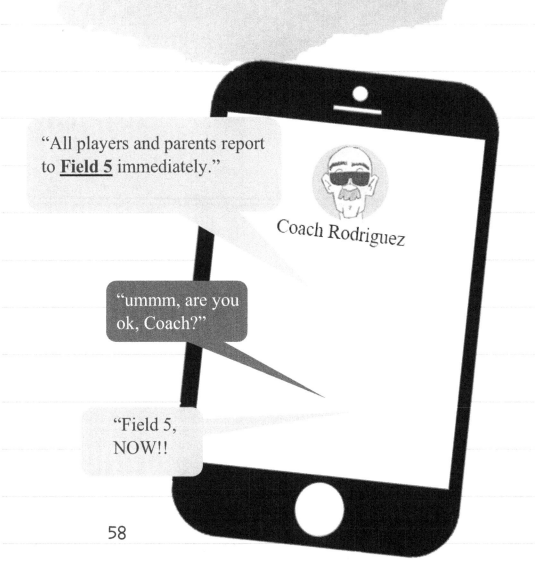

"All players and parents report to **Field 5** immediately."

Coach Rodriguez

"ummm, are you ok, Coach?"

"Field 5, NOW!!

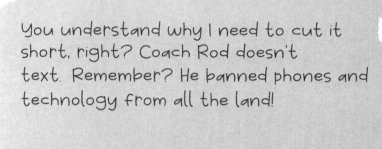

You understand why I need to cut it short, right? Coach Rod doesn't text. Remember? He banned phones and technology from all the land!

The world as we know it is coming to an end. I just know it!

Passing back to you, Kolt.

REEVES OUT

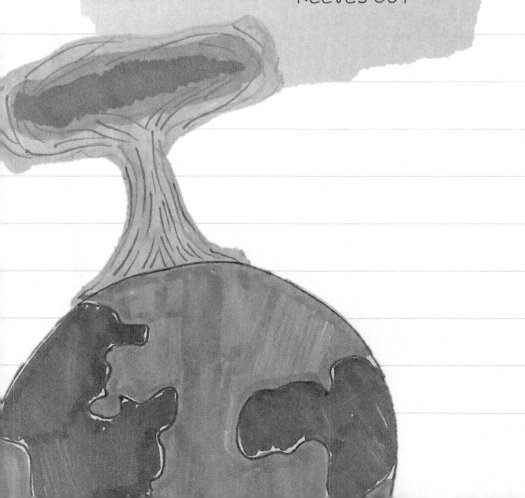

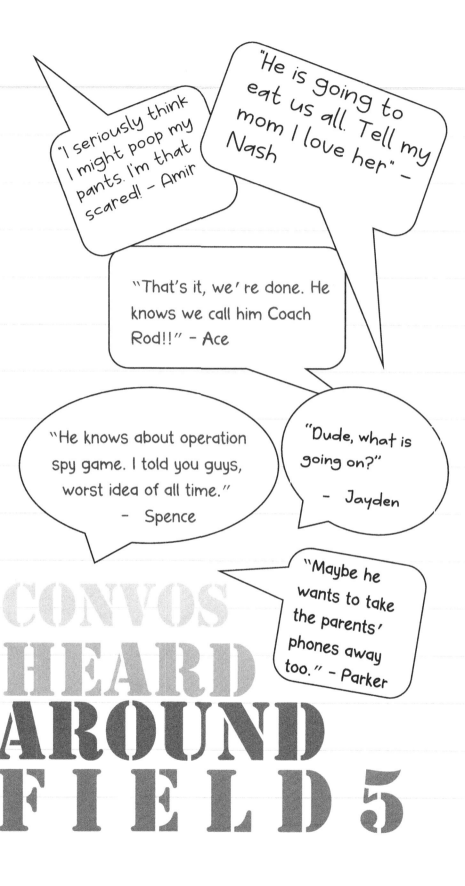

"Boys, I bring with some bad quit and playing

61

you here today news. Caleb he's for the...

KNIGHTS!

This is a betrayal of epic proportions. How could he do this?!?!

Shout out to Reeves for taking over Caleb's recap. He could have gotten away with our book. How awful would that be? Thanks for passing it back!

It is hard to process what is even happening! I need a minute or two here... Ok. Count back from 60 seconds.

Got it? I mean it!

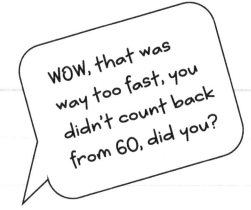

By the end of the meeting at Field 5 we learned:

-   We are a man short (Coach likes to keep
    a certain number of players on the team
    in case a sub is needed).

-   Caleb threw the game verse the Knights.
    It is the only thing that makes sense
    (even though he never said it). He wanted
    to leave the Bulldogs and hurt our record.

-   Spence can't find his stat book. He always
    leaves it in the front pocket of his
    backpack, but it is MISSING!!

64

Last time Spence had his stat book was at the end

of this game...

...and we couldn't shake the feeling that

someone was watching us. Even Spence asked me

to keep an eye on it during his at-bat.

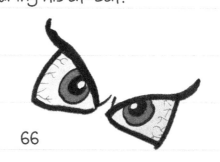

Somerville Game Schedule

✓ Home vs. Fish Street Sharks (June 1) (4 — 2 us)

✓ Home vs. Kingston Knights (June 9) (6 — 2 them)

(Away vs. Briardale Bandits (June 15))

Away vs. Slyville Foxes (June 22)

Home vs. Blue Rockets (June 29)

Away vs. South Philly Blazers (July 6)

Away vs. Green Devils (July 13)

Home vs. Pickleville Cucumbers (July 20)

Playoffs (teams to be determined)

$$\frac{2(8+6)}{2}$$

Entry Five
-briardale bandits-

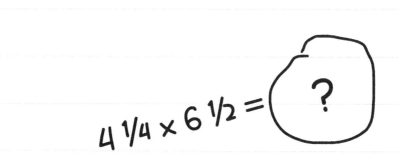
$$4\,\tfrac{1}{4} \times 6\,\tfrac{1}{2} = \boxed{?}$$

PLAYER of the GAME

SOMERVILLE Bulldogs

Spence Bryan
3rd base

46

Name: Spence 'Stats' Bryan

Saying:

"Never turn from the chance to

run bases or crunch numbers."

Check out my likes and dislikes. I ran a spreadsheet and

turned it into a pie chart for your viewing pleasure.

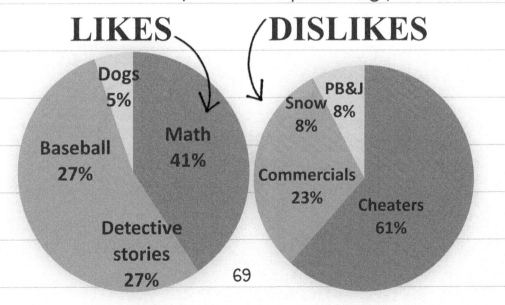

LIKES

- Dogs 5%
- Baseball 27%
- Math 41%
- Detective stories 27%

DISLIKES

- Snow 8%
- PB&J 8%
- Commercials 23%
- Cheaters 61%

69

recap:

vs. briardale bandits

June 15

> This is me, talking to myself!!
>
> HELLLPPP!

Don't panic!

Don't panic!!

Don't panic!!!

It has been a rough week and I am still processing

what happened on Field 5.

Still processing the fact that Caleb is a TRAITOR!

Still processing that my stats book is missing!

As for my recap, catch this... the week leading up to the

game was spent practicing grounders and pop-ups...

We were a man short with Caleb gone, so Quinn got called

up to practice with us!!! How awesome is that? Like

actually practice, not just watch like he's been doing!

We were so pumped for him!

Talk about
dedication, right?!

Today's game was against the Briardale Bandits.

I feel bad for them since their season is

pretty rocky, 0 and 3 (after our win against them

today). They kind of remind me of US from last year...

the season we DON'T talk about!

I hope they can turn it around. Maybe they need

a stats guy like me... After all – it was my math

skills that earned me player of the game.

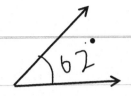

The numbers I computed in the dugout helped us

figure out the angles needed

to hit some major dingers!

All I had to do was figure out

the pitcher's velocity anndd....

never mind, I'll stop there.

It's not just geometry that makes a difference. Other

thing I keep tabs on are:

- Batting averages

- Fielding errors

- Pitch counts

- Unpaid snack bills

- Coach Rod's blood pressure

You know when you sit in math class and wonder, "when will I ever use this?!" Well— I am living proof that you can use math to help you out!!!

Unfortunately, I can't report to you the specifics

of our players since my stat book is still...

M-I-A

Missing. In. Action.

...instead, I'll tell you about some of my most

favorite random stats...

Stats -with- Spence

$$a^2 \times b^2 = C^2$$

FURTHEST HOME RUN

Furthest home run hit went to the SECOND deck of a stadium by a guy back in the 1980s. It soared almost 582 feet.

$$\frac{4(2+10)}{4}$$

ODDS OF BULLDOGS MAKING IT TO PLAYOFFS

Based on our percentage of wins this season and our batting averages, I predict an 80% chance of making it to the playoffs.

Odds of a bird pooping on you

- This depends on how many birds are in the area
- How many times birds fart and poop in an hour (the fart is crucial)
- How large your head is for the poop to land on (my little brother has a huge head- he's gotten pooped on twice)

WINNING THE LOTTERY

Likelihood of becoming a bazillionaire.

(less than 1%)

Jack's Special Request Orders

ORDER NUMBER   PLAYER NAME

08

OVERDUE

PAY UP

SNACK SHACK ODDS

The odds Parker will
ever pay off his Snack
Shack bill with Jack
(SLIM TO NONE)

Outstanding balance
of $98.56

DID YOU KNOW

Did you know there are 216
total stitches that cover
the seams on a baseball?

Man, I really hope I can find my book. Places I have

searched:

✓ Under my bed

✓ Bleachers at the baseball field

✓ In the dryer at home

✓ In between the couch cushions

✓ Under my brother's armpit

Yeah- you read that right.

I HAVE LOOKED EVERYWHERE!!!!!!!!!!!!!!!!

My teammates are going to help me look all over the

clubhouse and baseball fields. We are going to put up

"lost" flyers around Somerville too. You know what? I

could really use your help. Mind keeping an eye out too?

MISSING

Have you seen this notebook?

DESCRIPTION

Date missing: June 8

Identifying characteristics:
- Brown
- Pages with detailed baseball stats
- 'TOP SECRET' sticker x2 on front cover

Last seen at game versus the very sketchy Kingston Knights

REWARD
Endless sunflower seeds

Call or text with any information
215-123-4567
RETURN TO SOMERVILLE BULLDOGS BASEBALL

I also printed about 1000 copies to be handed out. Spread the word, people! I have to get started.

ELLIE WUZ HERE

<u>Somerville Game Schedule</u>

✓ Home vs. Fish Street Sharks (June 1) (4 — 2 us)

✓ Home vs. Kingston Knights (June 9) (6 — 2 them)

✓ Away vs. Briardale Bandits (June 15) (5 — 1 us)

~~Away vs. Slyville Foxes (June 22)~~

Home vs. Blue Rockets (June 29)

Away vs. South Philly Blazers (July 6)

Away vs. Green Devils (July 13)

Home vs. Pickleville Cucumbers (July 20)

Playoffs (teams to be determined)

I didn't no you had a diaree Jayden!! I found this under your bed. This is so boring. all it talks abut is baseball with your dorky friends. This needs some sprucing up.

Love and all that Jazz— Your Favorite Sister,

Ellie

Entry Six
-slyville foxes-

the little sister
TAKE OVER

PLAYER of the GAME

Name: Jayden Bell

Nicknames: Music Man, Sir-Sings-A-Lot

Did you know his middle name is MYRTLE?

Likes: Music, drawing (especially comics), crossword puzzles, belly flops (I feel NO PAIN!)

Dislikes: My little sister- Ellie (I don't not like her, she just follows me EVERYWHERE) and scary movies.

OMG. I DO NOT

81

recap:

vs. slyville foxes

June 22

Sum of my
fav stickerz →

Ellie

This is Princess Buttercup Unicorn. Her favorite things to do are fly in the sky, run across rainbows, and eat cotton candy.

Ellie Bell

My best puppies-
Moose &
Kimma

B.F.F.

Moose & Kimma
Bro & Sis

ATTENTION: ELLIE BELL

I cannot believe you wrote in this journal,

THEN actually glued that SUPER GIRLY picture of your insanely named unicorn in it,

THEN didn't say anything to me at dinner and pretended everything was normal.

ATTENTION: ELLIE BELL

This is for the BULLDOGS team eyes ONLY.

If you write one more word in here, I am going to tell mom... and you know how mad she gets if you go into my room!

Don't make me wake the dragon!!

Since my little sister rudely interrupted my recap

and wrote all over it (and I don't feel like re-writing it),

I'll keep it short.

WE WON

7-5

... and sent
those Slyville
Foxes
packing

Now, back to the rest of the week. Things got

very, very... I guess I'll say interesting.

It was Wednesday. We were meeting at the

batting cages for practice when we heard them...

The KINGSTON KNIGHTS.

They could not have made it any easier on us.

The Knights were spying in the same spot...

back by the train tracks. We heard Brendan yell

the secret word, "COCKA-DOODLE-DO" and then

we knew it was time. Turn to the next page to see

how we got REVENGE during...

Amir's Paint Balloon Palooza!

June 26

Jay-man,

That comic is awesome and is totally
accurate as to how we got sweet,
sweet revenge on the Knights.
Green paint was splattered all over
their measly bodies! I am still shocked
that THEY stole Spence's book.
STOLE, people, STOLE! They are tiny
thieves, committing crimes, and
spying on other baseball teams.

I wish it was the whole book we got
back and not just the one page, but
it is PROOF that they are the guilty
culprits. Let's take a team vote— do
we try to steal the book back?! Or
take EXTREME pleasure knowing
they will be stained GREEN for
weeks to come.

NO WAY
YES

On to the next game,

Brendan

extreme green pleasure
it is! Spence, we will help
ya start a new book

WAIT- WAIT- WAIT

Before we move on, we have to introduce our mascot! How have we gotten this far in the recaps without mentioning him?! Meet Bruce — the Backyard Bulldog

FUN FACTS:

- NAME: Bruce Diesel Power (yeah yeah, he has a first, middle, and last name!). The boys on the team call him by this when he is in trouble!!
- NICKNAMES (when not in trouble):
  - BD
  - BD Power
  - Sir snorts-a-lot
- AGE: 14 (is that dog years or human years, we don't know!)
- FAVORITE FOOD: Hot dogs, cheese steaks and ice cubes

Somerville Game Schedule

✓ Home vs. Fish Street Sharks (June 1)   (4 — 2 us)

✓ Home vs. Kingston Knights (June 9)   (6 — 2 them)

✓ Away vs. Briardale Bandits (June 15)   (5 — 1 us)

✓ Away vs. Slyville Foxes (June 22)   (7 — 5 us)

Home vs. Blue Rockets (June 29)

Away vs. South Philly Blazers (July 6)

Away vs. Green Devils (July 13)

Home vs. Pickleville Cucumbers (July 20)

Playoffs (teams to be determined)

Entry Seven
-blue rockets-

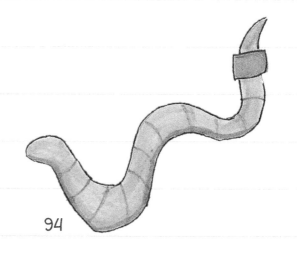

94

PLAYER of the game

SOMERVILLE Bulldogs

Kolten Ryan
pitcher

3

Nicknames:

- Kolt "The Bolt"

- Koko

My little bro calls me this

About Me

Likes: Babe Ruth, spaghetti and meatballs, striking people out, playing the guitar

Dislikes: Worms (which end is the head and which end is the butt?!?!?), vegetables, and walking people (a pitchers' worst nightmare)

recap:

vs. Blue Rockets

June 29

I'm the pitcher and I set the tone. If I can't throw strikes then... then what am I here for? I got the name Kolt "The Bolt" from Coach Q because I throw speeds like no other kid can! What happens, though, when you struggle on the pitching mound? Well, I will tell ya. You walk a lot of people.

The strike zone was NOT my friend today. To be honest, neither was the umpire (he needed new glasses!). Despite a bases loaded situation, we managed to get A big W due to some major defensive plays.

Final Score 5-1, Bulldogs.

As for Coach Rod, he was losing his mind the entire game. Throwing water bottles and screaming at parents. We weren't really sure why but his CRAZY antics have become the norm. Huffing and puffing like a crazed dragon.

Maybe if he was a little nicer, I would have told him about the most disgusting...

...totally gross piece of food stuck in his...

Breaking news!!!

EXTRA, EXTRA

READ ALL ABOUT IT!

Issue #2

Stop what you are doing, put everything down.

We interrupt this journal recap for

ANOTHER BREAKING MUSTACHE REPORT

The following is based on mysteries discovered in Coach Rod's furry mustache too horrific to keep to ourselves.

The items found are terrible, strange, and sometimes unbelievable. Everything you read is completely true and not exaggerated at all. Except for the parts we totally made up.

Have your favorite blankie or stuffy ready. We will not be held liable for nightmares. You've been warned.

BREAKING MUSTACHE REPORT

(AGAIN!!!!)

Issue #2

What you are about to read is one of the GREATEST mysteries on Earth. Right up there with the existence of Big Foot, aliens, and mayonnaise.

During the game today, Coach Rod had the biggest piece of SARDINE stuck in his mustache. And not like a full sardine, but the actual head of one.

What is a SARDINE you may be wondering? For those who don't know (consider yourself LUCKY)- a SARDINE is a small, smelly fish that people eat (yeah- you read that right).

People eat them in sandwiches...with chicken. This may be hard to imagine BUT people will even eat them OUT OF A CAN. Almost like how people eat chips out of bag. But chips I can understand. They are salty, AMAZINGINESS.

99

BREAKING MUSTACHE REPORT
(AGAIN!!!!)

Issue #2

People also use them as PIZZA TOPPINGS (something so wrong it should be considered ILLEGAL). The only pizza toppings that should be allowed are as follows:

- Pepperoni
- Pepper
- Sausage
- Pineapple

You tell me- did Coach Rod break the unwritten law by getting a grotesque SARDINE stuck in his mustache because he ate it as a pizza topping?

Or is he PURPOSELY keeping the head of this poor, smelly fish in his mustache as a reminder to what he does to his enemies?

Will he top this week's mystery mustache food?! Only time will tell…. Until then, we are officially GROSSED OUT!

Man - I love mustache reports. They make me laugh. A LOT.

Imagine how mad "THE ROD-STER" would be if he knew

they existed - luckily, he doesn't have a clue!

Something just as important as the mustache report,

OUR WINNING RECORD (this 5-1 win was HUGE). The parents

thought it would be a good idea to celebrate such an

achievement with a block party!!!

No, no, no. Not this
kind of block!!

101

If you never heard of a block party, boy - you are in for a treat! A block party is a giant neighborhood celebration when everyone on the block comes together to party.

The best part is the streets get blocked off and shut down so cars can NOT drive through. Letting kids run all over the place and ride bikes all over the street taking over the neighborhood for one awesome night.

Block parties in the summer are the best!

Things we did at this year's party:

- Water balloon toss

- Rode bikes — all day

- Stick Ball

- Egg toss

- Danced to the DJ

Funniest moment:

The DJ played our favorite song. Parker grabbed the microphone and sung along for everyone to hear.

I ran and grabbed my guitar and just like that we were having a concert and dance party!

Let's play – TAKE A WILD GUESS!

RULES: Listed below are dance moves... was it a parent or a kid rocking out? Check off who you think... I will go first.

Dance move	Parent	-OR-	Kid
The Floss	✓		
Electric Slide			✓
Whip & Nae Nae	✓		
Chicken dance			✓
The Griddy	✓		
The Tootsie Roll	✓		
Cha-Cha Slide			✓
Cupid Shuffle			

The block party was wild and fun! It will definitely be added to Jack's list as one of the top days of the year!!

Somerville Game Schedule

✓ Home vs. Fish Street Sharks (June 1)   (4 – 2 us)

✓ Home vs. Kingston Knights (June 9)   (6 – 2 them)

✓ Away vs. Briardale Bandits (June 15)   (4 – 1 us)

✓ Away vs. Slyville Foxes (June 22)   (7 – 5 us)

✓ Home vs. Blue Rockets (June 29)   (5 – 1 us)

Away vs. South Philly Blazers (July 6)

Away vs. Green Devils (July 13)

Home vs. Pickleville Cucumbers (July 20)

Playoffs (teams to be determined)

Entry Eight
-philly blazers-

PLAYER of the game

Brendan Banks
1st base
34
SOMERVILLE Bulldogs

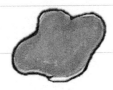

Name: Brendan Banks

Position: 1st base babbbyyyy

ALL ABOUT ME

Likes: The beach, PB & J (hold the crust), and

riding my bike

Dislikes: Cleaning my room (just about the

worst thing ever) and homework.

recap:

vs. Philly Blazers

July 6

Those Philly Blazers gave us one heck of a run.

I somehow got player of the game. Before I tell you

who it should have gone to, let me recap the

wildest game of my life.

It started like any other game. Coaches and

captains in the huddle, national anthem sung

by Amir's mom, and the ump yelling our two

favorite words...

"PLAY BALL!"

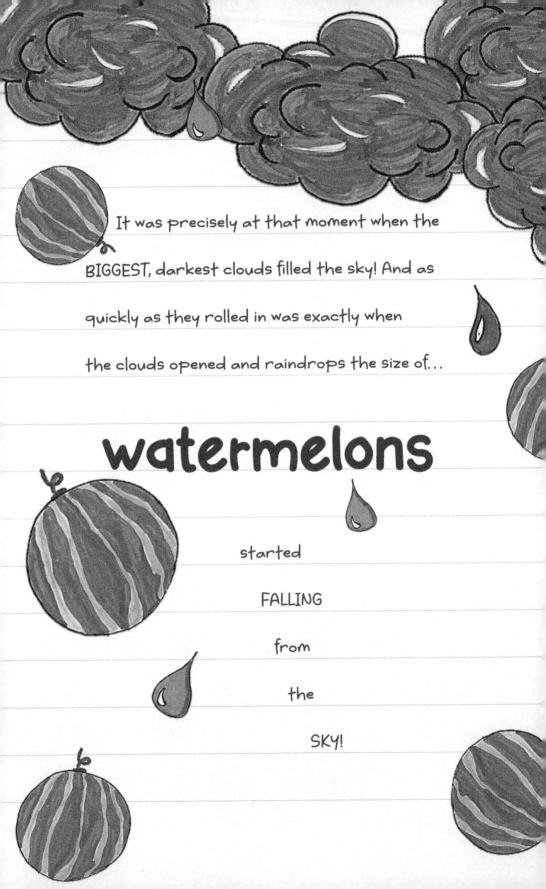

It was precisely at that moment when the BIGGEST, darkest clouds filled the sky! And as quickly as they rolled in was exactly when the clouds opened and raindrops the size of...

watermelons

started

FALLING

from

the

SKY!

Ace was up to bat first. He swung and slipped

right into the mud — instantly covered from

head to toe. It looked like poop all over his face.

It was so thick he had to wipe the ~~poop~~ — OOPs -

I mean mud, away from his eyes so he could

see the next pitch.

AND THEN-WOOSHHH. Same thing! It looked like

instant replay. It was

identical. And just like

that, the ump yelled

our two least favorite

words...

"RAIN DELAY"

While the other team retreated to their cars, the

Somerville Bulldogs (parents included) took advantage

of the rain!! With some grit and imagination, the

baseball field transformed into the most

ultimate

slip and slide

EVER!!!

WARNING - I can't draw good at all, so you have

to use your imagination with the picture to the right.

Imagine it looks like the coolest baseball field, ever,

overflowing in water. So much that the baselines turned

into a slip and slide.

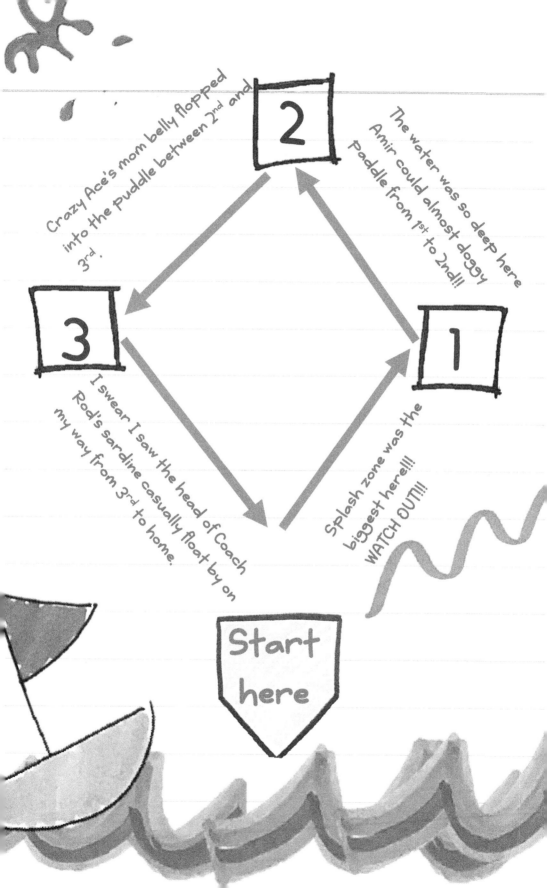

ONE WAY TO PHILLY

Shortly after our antics, the skies cleared, the sun started to shine, and the game began.

Our adrenaline from the biggest slip and slide NEVER ended. We whoooooped the Philly Blazers behinds, and sent them back to a far, far away land called South Philadelphia.

"behind" is a clever word for BUTT

ha ha ha-
that says BUTT

SOMERVILLE Bulldogs

Nash Walker
short stop

15

That brings us back to my original thought... why the player of the game needs to to go to this guy, NASH!

My man showed up to play and sealed the

deal at the end of the game with a mighty

grand slam

soaring the score to 7 — 3, Bulldogs. So I'd like

to dedicate this recap to my best friend,

NASH the Smash, the toughest kid in town.

Nash, this one's for you!

South Philly is known for their cheesesteaks, maybe they can bring us one back if we face them again.

For Brendan's eyes only!

Dear Brendan— That may be the nicest thing anyone has ever done for me. Sharing YOUR recap. Even nicer than my big bro giving me the last slice of pizza last week.

There's a reason they call us the unstoppable Bash Bro's

BREDAN
+ NASH
BASH

Let me tell you something, this is also the reason why I hate common core math and algebra (there should just not be letters in math, COME ON PEOPLE)!

You know what, as a thank you— your next pack of gum is on me!

From one half of the BASH BRO'S,

Nash

Jack's Special Request Orders

ORDER NUMBER

34

PLAYER NAME

Nash Smash

Bubble gum. (50 pieces)

$3.25

Some of the juiciest, most bubbly pieces of bubble gum you got Jack. Please bring to next game for my guy Brendan

- Nash

Somerville Game Schedule

✓ Home vs. Fish Street Sharks (June 1)   (4 — 2 us)

✓ Home vs. Kingston Knights (June 9)   (6 — 2 them)

✓ Away vs. Briardale Bandits (June 15)   (4 — 1 us)

✓ Away vs. Slyville Foxes (June 22)   (7 — 5 us)

✓ Home vs. Blue Rockets (June 29)   (5 — 1 us)

✓ Away vs. South Philly Blazers (July 6)   (7 — 3 us)

Away vs. Green Devils (July 13)

Home vs. Pickleville Cucumbers (July 20)

Playoffs (teams to be determined)

117

Entry Nine

-green devils-

PLAYER of the game

SOMERVILLE Bulldogs

Henry Koin
Back up 1st & 2nd

20

Name: Henry Koin

Fun Fact: I'm the only one

in my family with red hair

LIKES

- High top sneakers
- Winter (sledding is a blast!!)
- Snow days (duh, you get to sled!)
- Hot chocolate WITH marshmallows

disLIKES

- Sitting in traffic with my dad
- Listening to my dad sing in the car (with the windows down!)
- The feeling of sand in flip flops, EWWW
- Nosepickers

RECAP:

VS. GREEN DEVILS

July 13

This one <u>HURT</u>. It was our second loss of the

season to the Green Devils and man — it was a

devilish loss. We played a bad game. Our running

was slow; so slow that Coach Rod checked our

spikes for bricks!

Then he LAUNCHED Amir's

spikes into outer space. The

parents gasped. I am still in

shock.

In case you were wondering, the stats book is still missing, too!

STILL MISSING

Areas we checked:

- Under the bases
- All baseball bags
- The pizza shop
- EVERYWHERE!!!!

It is pretty clear the Knights don't know anything about sportsmanship. You know, since they stole our stat book and all. But I will tell you who does, Quinn! That kid is always POSITIVE!

We need kids like Quinn to keep the team spirit up.

Those guys are just as important as the best

players on the team!

Lucky for us, Quinn is on the practice squad now

and he is killlllling it! Kolt and Jack have really

stepped up and helped him a lot. They stay after

practice to work on grounders and hitting.

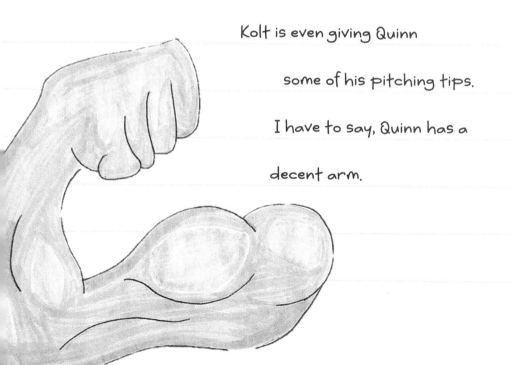

Kolt is even giving Quinn

some of his pitching tips.

I have to say, Quinn has a

decent arm.

WWWoooowwww! It is happening AGAIN! Like as I write this recap. Coach Rod is texting the parents, AGAIN!

"All players report to Field 5, NOW!!!"

this is not a drill

Ok, let's go check out what's happening at Field 5.

"He knows about the journal and has come to eat the pages..."

– Ace

"My feet are freezing, think he bought me a new pair of shoes?!" -Henry

"I think we need to play the lottery- the odds of him texting twice in one season are more unlikely than winning a million $$"

- Spence

He didn't eat us last time, so this has to be it! Tell my mom I love her... again." – Nash

"One word. Sus." – Jack

CONVOS HEARD AROUND FIELD 5

"Boys, Quinn working hard a spot on

has been
and earned
the..."

Somerville Bulldog ROSTER!

By the end of the meeting at Field 5 we learned:

- Quinn will come to the next game in his Bulldog uniform!

- Not to be fooled by Coach Rod's "nice" gesture. He is still INSANE and made us run a million laps for losing the game.

- We have a GREAT record (even with this loss) - we *should* be set for playoffs IF we can win the next game.

Someone pinch me- I must be dreaming... us, the Bulldogs, a chance at the Playoffs!

pinch!!

OUCH- I can't believe you really did that. You know it is just an expression- right?!

Somerville Game Schedule

✓ Home vs. Fish Street Sharks (June 1)   (4 – 2 us)

✓ Home vs. Kingston Knights (June 9)   (6 – 2 them)

✓ Away vs. Briardale Bandits (June 15)   (4 – 1 us)

✓ Away vs. Slyville Foxes (June 22)   (7 – 5 us)

✓ Home vs. Blue Rockets (June 29)   (5 – 1 us)

✓ Away vs. South Philly Blazers (July 6)   (7 – 3 us)

Away vs. Green Devils (July 13)   (3-2 them)

Home vs. Pickleville Cucumbers (July 20)

Playoffs (teams to be determined)

Entry Ten
-pickleville cucumbers-

PLAYER of the game

THE PRANKSTER

SOMERVILLE Bulldogs

Amir Youssef
2nd base
82

Favorite MLB player:

KEN GRIFFEY, JR (G.O.A.T)

When I get older I want to be an ump for the

major league! We have the funniest ump at our games.

He loves to dance as he calls people out! I think it's

about time some of those moves make it to the majors

too!

-LIKES/disLIKES-

I love trading baseball cards, going to the movies and
eating cereal for dinner (do not get me started on my
dads cooking- woof). But I absolutely HATE cats, going to
the doctors, and my dads cooking.

Remember: dinner + cereal = my favorite

recap:

vs. Pickleville Cucumbers

July 20

BIG win today!

We chopped up the Pickleville Cucumbers and won

the game 12 to 3. Literally chopped them up like

little pieces of pickle-ish cucumbers — sprinkled

everywhere on the field. Like confetti thrown at a

surprise party!!!!

This was the win we needed.

WE MADE IT TO

PLAYOFFS

Between the smelly pits of last season and our bumps

in the road this year, I never thought we'd make it this

far, but we did! Playoffs - here we come!! The new,

improved, and totally old-school, journal passing

Somerville Bulldogs! Let's pass the journal around and

get some ideas on how we can prepare for playoffs.

We've never been here before-

...we need a plan

...like a really good plan.

And now I have to ask my mom to cut up

some cucumbers. I have a sudden craving.

July 21

Dear Somerville Slugger Fam,

Let's think about who we will be up against.

Starting tomorrow night- the Blue Rockets are facing the Browny Buckeyes at 6:00PM. Night game, under the big lights! Let's go and watch their game, as a team. Whoever comes out with the win will be our first-round playoff match.

Bring your notepads, sunflower seeds, and thinking caps because we need to become the best scouts in town and get ready for our next baseball game!

What do you thin'

From, Amir

Count me in too!
- Amir & Ace

July 23

Yo Team —

LAST NIGHTS GAME WAS WILD.

I do not even know what to say....

I can't believe the Blue Rockets hit a walk off homer to beat the Buckeyes. EPIC. No explanation can do it justice!

Let's throw our notes together and see what observations we made about our upcoming opponents, the Rockets.

From,
Brendan

Countdown to Playoffs in 10, 9, 8 ...

ADD SCOUTING REPORTS HERE:

Rockets know how to swing the bat. May not always make contact, but they still swing for the fences.

Their third batter, Bryce Cruz, had a walk off homerun to win the game. We are gonna need to throw that kid the heat and try to strike him out.

CRAZY CRAZY PARENTS

Blue Rockets sure have some fast feet, those kids can steal bases!

Jack's Special Request Or

ORDER NUMBER   PLAYER NAME

They don't always field great. missed some easy outs here and there.

Parker- you owe me for your order of funnel fries- pay up before next weeks practice...

LITTLE LEAGUE

Now that we know all the teams heading into the playoffs, here is what the schedule looks like...

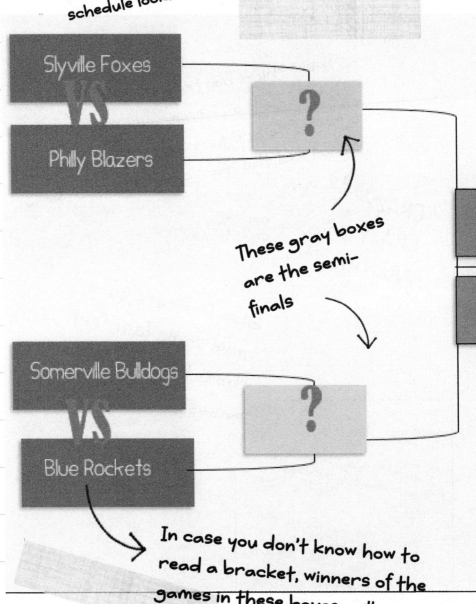

Slyville Foxes

VS

Philly Blazers

?

These gray boxes are the semi-finals

Somerville Bulldogs

VS

Blue Rockets

?

In case you don't know how to read a bracket, winners of the games in these boxes will advance to the semi-finals

PLAYOFF BRACKET

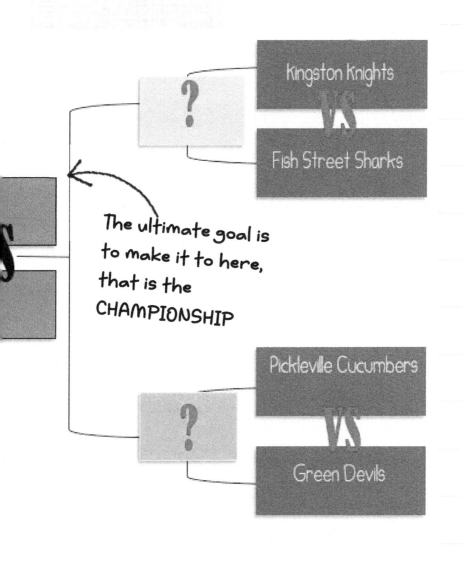

Kingston Knights

VS

Fish Street Sharks

?

The ultimate goal is to make it to here, that is the CHAMPIONSHIP

Pickleville Cucumbers

VS

Green Devils

?

Somerville Game Schedule

✓ Home vs. Fish Street Sharks (June 1)   (4 — 2 us)

↓ Home vs. Kingston Knights (June 9)   (6 — 2 them)

✓ Away vs. Briardale Bandits (June 15)   (4 — 1 us)

✓ Away vs. Slyville Foxes (June 22)   (7 — 5 us)

✓ Home vs. Blue Rockets (June 29)   (5 — 1 us)

✓ Away vs. South Philly Blazers (July 6)   (7 — 3 us)

✓ Away vs. Green Devils (July 13)   (3-2 them)

Home vs. Pickleville Cucumbers (July 20) (12 — 3 us)

Playoffs (teams to be determined)

Holy cow, holy cow, holy cow.

This is it.

Entry Eleven
-playoffs-
blue rockets

I'm taking over the recaps from here. Coach Q said there are no more Players-of-the-Game. It's all about teamwork from here on out.

-Kolten

Playoff recap:
vs. Blue Rockets

July 27

This past week was the hardest week EVER! Before the

birds started chirping in the morning, we were already

up, making our way to the fields in the heat of the summer.

Every waking, SWEATING moment was spent:

- Thinking about baseball

- Playing baseball

- Watching baseball

By the end of the week, we were as tired as:

- A turtle racing a rabbit

- The sole of a worn-out shoe

But when it came to game time, it was plain and simple We SMOKED the Blue Rockets. Whooped.

Mainly because our scouting reports were AMAZING. We knew exactly what to expect. We knew they Swing for the fences - so our outfielders played deep.

We were ready for their stud, Bryce Cruz... we purposely walked him (not a move I like, but we were playing to win). We also knew their parents were nuts, so we packed ear plugs. You can say our scouting reports paid off and won us the game!!

We weren't going to let our first playoff WIN slip by - we headed back to Jack's house. Here, every Somerville snackity-snack could be found.

To understand Somerville food, you need to understand

geography (and if you're like me – you hate geography).

So, instead of rambling on and on about the yummy

delicious snacks, check out the "snack

map" of Somerville on the next page

and see some of the foods we got

to enjoy.

Be careful!

You may start

to drool (the food

is just that good).

City of
Somerville Love

 If you live here, we call this 'W-0-0-D-E-R I-C-E'

 Home of 'Mini Melts' Tiny little ice cream morsels that melt in your mouth, practically turning into a milkshake.

Northeast

North

Center City

 Wiz or American? Wit or witout? That's the only way we do it.

West

South

 You haven't had a pretzel until you tried a Somerville soft pretzel. Doughy, warm and so, so good!

This has nothing to do with food; but here in Somerville, we are also known for a famous boxer that loved to run stairs for some strange

We stuffed our faces with food and then went to the

pool - cannon balls, belly flops, and

Mini Melts Ice Cream EVERYWHERE. My type of

pool party - until Jack's mom yelled,

"OUT OF THE POOL -
PRONTO! Don't you
know the rule? You
have to wait 30
minutes to swim
after eating!"

I have never

heard of such

nonsense -

neither has the rest of

the team. We turned the music up,

and kept the belly flops going...

After a lot of partying, it was time to focus on

what we came to do this season. Take a look at the

most up-to-date standings.

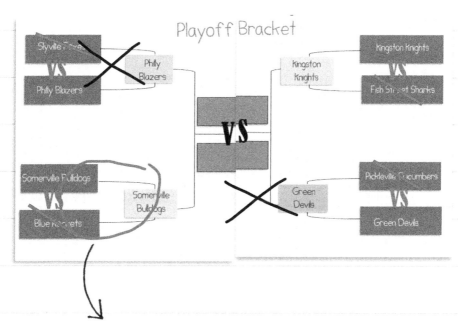

Can you believe it? We are advancing to the semi-finals

and will verse the Philly Blazers (we played them

before and won - but it was close!). There is something

about these guys - I don't know what it is... I'll be

keeping an eye on them!

Somerville Game Schedule

Home vs. Fish Street Sharks (June 1)   (4 — 2 us)

Home vs. Kingston Knights (June 9)   (6 — 2 them)

Away vs. Briardale Bandits (June 15)   (4 — 1 us)

Away vs. Slyville Foxes (June 22)   (7 — 5 us)

Home vs. Blue Rockets (June 29)   (5 — 1 us)

Away vs. South Philly Blazers (July 6)   (7 — 3 us)

Away vs. Green Devils (July 13)   (3-2 them)

Home vs. Pickleville Cucumbers (July 20) (12 — 3 us)

Playoffs (teams to be determined)

SEMI FINALS

Dude - hate to admit it, butttttttt JACK'S
MOM WAS RIGHT!

Non -stop burps, wet farts, and belly bubbles.

NEVER. EATING. BEFORE. SWIMMING.
AGAIN.

147

Entry Twelve

-semifinals-

philly blazers

July 30

Last night's game versus the Blazers was UNBELIEVABLE.

For starters, the fans were wild and crazy. Teams from

all over the league came to watch this game — even

the Kingston Knights were in attendance. It was standing

room only at Field 5 in Somerville.

Our parents made signs and decorated the stands with

streamers. Pictures of bulldogs were stapled to poles

and our favorite warm-up songs were blaring loudly

over the speakers (so loud we could feel the songs

vibrate our bodies!)

It felt like we were playing in the World Series!

Lightning bugs flashed in the sky making it look

like millions of cameras were taking our picture.

All of this — the sold-out crowd... the cheering

fans... the music...

I wanted to remember this

moment forever! The

feeling right before the

game started... so

I snuck my mom's camera

and took a picture.

Hey batter batter!

Rumor has it some people call these things fireflies... can you imagine?! They are lightning bugs people! Come on!

FINALLY, we heard the umpire call, "Five minutes until first pitch, five minutes until first pitch." The coaches called us in... it was time for THE pep talk. We got into the huddle. The crowd went silent. Even Mrs. Layton's newborn baby stopped crying. Coach Q said,

"Take a look around boys, breathe this moment in...

Remember this feeling.

Remember this image.

This is why we have worked so hard.

This is why we do what we do.

For this feeling, this experience.

You are the boys of Somerville.

Make those South Philly boys never forget who you are."

SUDDENLY

We heard someone yelling. I scanned the

bleachers quickly – only to see the one, the only –

Gerald Pickle. Gerald Pickle from the rotten Knights

was holding an old school megaphone in the air!

Sirens were blasting from the horn, startling

Mrs. Layton's hushed baby.

Gerald looked at me; he had fire in his eyes. Smoke

was just about to erupt from his ears when he

yelled,

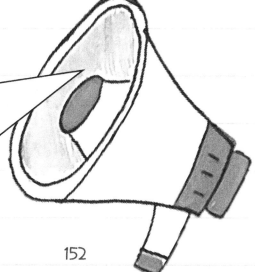

"Those Philly Blazers are a bunch of cheating losers! They don't deserve to be playing in the semi-finals."

The crowd, again, went silent. You could hear a pin drop.

Gerald Pickle, oh boy, that Gerald pickle... he really

came with the mic drop. Although I heard the words

come out of his   mouth — my brain could

not process what

he said. I

only

caught

parts and

it went

like this:

- The Kingston Knights have never
  spied on a baseball practice of
  ours. BUT players on the Blazers
  dressed as the Knights did. Making
  us think it was the Knights spying
  every Wednesday

- The Knights also thought that WE
  (as in Somerville) were cheaters
  too! The Philly Blazers did the same
  thing at their practices but
  dressed as us!

- Which means, the Kingston Knights
  never stole Spence's stat book, but
  the Philly Blazers did!

At first, none of us believed Gerald Pickle. It simply could **not** be true. The Kingston Knights were cheaters Brendan caught them a couple weeks ago at practice. Remember, we even deployed Amir's Balloon Palooza as payback.

We got them so good that there was NO WAY they could wash away ALL the GREEN paint that stained their skin...

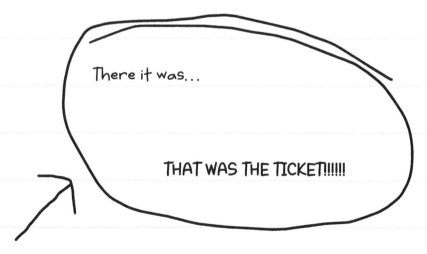

There it was...

THAT WAS THE TICKET!!!!!!

154

Nash marched over to the Kingston Knights, who were in

the stands, and demanded they show us their hands.

I wouldn't believe it if I didn't see it with my own eyes.

NOT one ounce of GREEN was spotted on any team

member of the Knights. Not a dot... Not a spec...

Not a single crumb of GREEN left under a fingernail

to be seen. This could only mean ONE thing...

Nash ran, FAST, to the Blazers dugout and ripped

off a player's batting glove. Weird... EVERY player was

wearing gloves. The look on Nash's face said it all!

He saw the GREEN stained hands of Aiden Buck.

The Kingston Knights were not the team spying, they weren't the bad guys. We had it all wrong, AFTER ALL THIS TIME... It was the Philly Blazers!!!

Nash took a deep breath. Turned. Walked directly to Gerald Pickle and the rest of the Knights...

"Knights: On behalf of my team, we owe you an apology- we're sorry. It looks like the Blazers pulled a fast one on us... on both of us."

It suddenly felt like a scene from a movie. The bleachers started to make a thunderous sound.

It was the Knights stomping their feet — over and over! They chanted, "Bulldogs, Bulldogs, Bulldogs!" I even spotted Caleb — stomping, chanting (and smiling) with his new team.

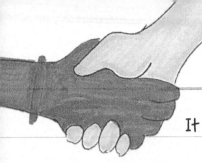

It was at that moment... The feud between the Kingston Knights and Somerville Bulldogs ended. The crowd continued to roar with excitement and the umpire yelled, "PLAY BALL!"

We did exactly that.

The game was neck and neck.

If the Bulldogs scored, the Blazers answered. By the end of the eighth inning we were tied, 3-3. It was clear we were all exhausted... eye black smeared down our faces, sweat soaked our hats. The score remained the same at the top of the ninth; 3-3.

Then, it was our turn to bat. *This was our moment!*

It came down to Parker "The Fridge" Reeves.

INSERT DRAMATIC BATMAN VOICE.

PARKER SWUNG.

HIT.

THE BALL BOUNCED.

THE CENTER FIELDER ROUNDED THE BALL.

PARKER CRUISED PASSED 2nd BASE.

THE CENTER FIELDER THREW FOR 3RD

PARKER WAS GOING TO BE OUT.

THEN KARMA STRUCK. ———

Karma is some sort of fate or destiny when good things happen for doing good or bad things happen for doing bad. Like what goes around comes around.

THEY. DROPPED. THE. BALL.

158

With nothing to lose and
everything to gain...
Parker darted from
third and headed to
home plate!

That is the story of how we advanced to the

Little League

BASEBALL CHAMPIONSHIP

Sing it with me now

We going... we going

We going to the CHIP

WHAT?

WE GOING TO THE CHIP

Not like a Potato chip. That would be weird.

Let me explain...

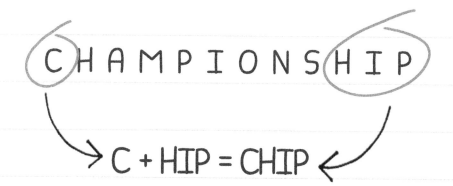

C H A M P I O N S H I P

C + HIP = CHIP

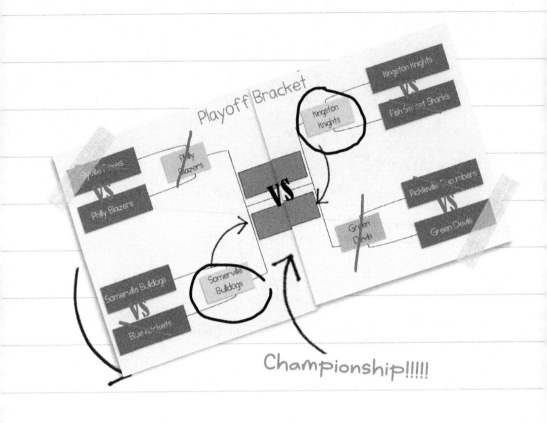

Playoff Bracket

Skyville Doves

Philly Blazers

Philly Blazers

Somerville Bulldogs

Blue Rockets

Somerville Bulldogs

VS

Kingston Knights

Fish Street Sharks

Kingston Knights

Pickleville Cucumbers

Green Devils

Green Devils

Championship!!!!!

Entry Thirteen
-championship-
kingston knights

August 2

Three days and counting until the biggest day of

our lives: The Championship. We are so excited to have

gotten this far, but preparing for the Chip just doesn't

feel the way we expected it to.

Decades of pointless feuds and stress — for what?

Both of our teams — Bulldogs and Knights — we were:

- scammed

- duped

- tricked

- fooled

- hoodwinked

Did you know there were that many words for cheated?!

We were played like fools.

We don't want to be rivals anymore!
it feels silly and tiring... very, very
tiring! I only know of the long,
feuding history of the Knights and
Bulldogs from my Grand Father, Pop-Pop Ryan.

He was a Somerville baseball player when he was
a kid. The pranks originated way back then.

The moment I heard the news from Gerald Pickle,
I knew what I had to do. Pop can't come to games
anymore, so after, I booked it to his house to tell
him what we learned. He shook his head so hard in
disbelief. His dentures actually
fell out of his mouth!!

I laughed. And I laughed. And I laughed some more.

I may have laughed until I farted.

FARTED LOUD. The truest sign of a good laugh.

I laughed all the way home!

I couldn't even make it upstairs I was so tired

from laughing. So, I passed out on my living room

couch.

August 3

I had a dream last night...

Both teams (Knights and Bulldogs) came together to take down the Philly Blazers with an epic prank. It was only a dream, but I woke up with the biggest smile.

That smile carried me all the way to practice on

a totally new field...

"The Marinucci Park Baseball Stadium"

This place is the real deal. We'll play the

Championship on that field tomorrow. Rumor has

it legends played there.

Can't wait to be a part of legendary history tomorrow

when we take down the Knights.

August 4

I said I was going to finish off the journal recaps and

tell you how the rest of our season went down. I said

there wouldn't be another "player of the game" because

Coach Rod said we all had to be in this together for

the playoffs.　　　　　　　　　　Some promises are
　　　　　　　　　　　　　　　　just meant to be
　　　　　　　　　　　　　　　　　　broken!

BUT there is no way I will take the final recap away

from this guy... It has to come from him...

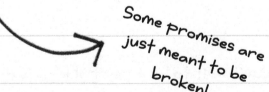

PLAYER of the
championship

Not an official picture since I wasn't on the team at first... this is a pic my dad grabbed after the big game. Usually, my uniform is pristine. But I will tell you this – I EARNED THIS DIRTY UNIFORM.

Quinn Reed
'the back up'

-LIKES-

- Being on the practice squad
- Grounders
- The Coaches!
- Mac & Cheese

-disLIKES-

- Bullies (go bother someone else, will ya?!)
- Winter (that means NO baseball)
- Putting my cleats on

I told my mom about this notebook - how the players were writing recaps of the games. I always wondered what stories and secrets it held. Let me tell you, this thing is awesome! I named it 'Journal of The Backyard Kids' and everyone on the team loved it!

We are all one big family. This neighborhood, this team. We are all Backyard Kids. I guess you could say...

We are all Backyard Bulldogs.

Kolt told me I get to write the final entry because I deserve it. I'm so nervous. I don't want to mess this up.

Me... Quinn... the kid who didn't even make the team.

Writing the final recap for our season.

This is AWESOME! Here goes nothing...

PRESS THIS BUTTON to activate gameday flashbacks

The game went like this - first seven innings; NOTHING

- Absolutely nothing.

- Not a hit.

- Not a run.

- Not even a forced walk.

It was boring.

Even the ump fell asleep behind the plate!

All of that changed during the 7th inning stretch

- "Take Me Out to The Ball Game" played over the

  speakers

- Mascots frolicked around pumping up the fans

  (nobody saw the diabolical madness that was

  about to unfold)

COMMENCE:
Operation Bubble Gum Cannon

What is the purpose of 'Operation Bubble Gum Cannon?'

To team up with the Knights and seek the ultimate revenge on the Blazers.

A play-by-play of how this dangerous undercover mission occurred is listed on the next page.

- Mascots (who were in on the prank) aimed prize cannons filled with bubble gum to the absolute worst spot in the stands. The section where the Blazers sat!

- The mascots pushed a button that launched gum into the stands. There was so much bubble gum loaded, it looked like the sky was painted pink.

- The Blazers jumped for joy. They totally took the bait and started to chew.... They chewed and chewed until they started to blow the biggest bubbles. They chewed until...

- **POP**, they were COVERED in gum.

Little did they know, this was not ordinary gum

Amir preloaded the prize cannon with a top-secret prank gum filled with glue. Once popped, anything the glue touched would be stuck together for 30 minutes.

- You better believe The Blazers were stuck in place, on the stands. They couldn't move a muscle.

- <u>ACTIVATE</u> Little sister take over part 2.
  - ○ Ellie Bell (remember, Jayden's sis) and the other little kids sprinkled glitter and confetti all over the Blazers and bedazzled them. Some even went so far to draw mustaches on them! With all that glue and glitter, they are going to
    look like disco balls for days!

- Amir snapped a photo or two as evidence.

It was epic.
~~It went as planned.~~

But Poor, poor Amir. He just had to get that
picture. He slipped on the bleachers and fell...
getting stuck in his own trap!! He couldn't
budge. He was stuck like a statue in the gum
with the sticky, stinky Blazers.

We panicked, he wiggled.
We huddled, he grunted.
We needed Amir at second base, but he was
stuck like the lid on a cookie jar.

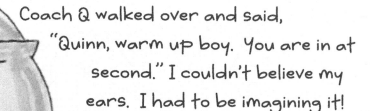

Coach Q walked over and said,
"Quinn, warm up boy. You are in at
second." I couldn't believe my
ears. I had to be imagining it!

But then I suddenly felt my teammates surround me, jumping up and down. I knew my moment had finally arrived.

The excitement of the 7th inning stretch dwindled and we were back to the boring old championship game. Until the bottom of the 9th. Still tied 0 - 0, it was my turn at the plate.

My heart felt like it was in my throat, my knees were rattling (this may be the most important at-bat, EVER!!).

SWOOOOOOOOooooooooooOOOOOOSSHHHH

A pitch came blazing right down the center, and it was about to cross home plate... I took a deep breath. It was as if the world was moving in slow motion. I closed my eyes....

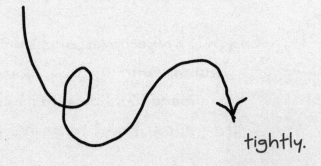

tightly.

I thought back... Back to what I learned this season. What it meant to be part of a team.

- I remembered Brendan and Nash with their arms stretched - pulling me out of the dumpster during 'Operation Spy Game'.

- I envisioned Parker ripping a homer to win the game against the Philly Blazers.

- I laughed every time Coach Rod ended up with a mysterious item in his mustache.

- I saw my teammates come together to erase a historical rivalry that was decades old.

Then, I took a huge step and swung with all my might. The bat went **CRACK**. I felt a jolt that moved up my arms and into the universe. I saw the outfield scurry.

I ran as fast as I could to first base.

I heard the announcer over the loudspeaker say,

"That ball is going. Man, that ball is going. That ball is...

outtttta here!!!"

The crowd ROARED with excitement.

I didn't know what was happening — but my feet
took me for a ride around the bases. As I rounded
third for home, I saw the Somerville Bulldogs
waiting for ME - QUINN STINKING REED — to get
to home plate.

We jumped, we hugged, we dog piled. The parents
cried, the fans shouted, the little sisters rushed
the field.

Coach Q huddled us in... and in typical Q fashion,
he made us appreciate the moment. He gave us
one of those speeches that are made for the
movies. The kind where dramatic music plays in the
background, and you feel like NOTHING (and I mean
NOTHING) can hold you back.

And when he was done, like clockwork, we started to chant "Rise Up... Rise Up... Rise Up..." Coach Rod cleared his throat, but words wouldn't come out.

He looked like he was going to choke...

...uh oh - we killed Coach Rod.

What the heck is happening?!
It wasn't supposed to end this way...

JUST KIDDING. But something totally
unexpected did happen.

Coach Rod smiled... (the biggest smile).

And kept on smiling as
   ONE
      HUGE
         SINGLE
            TEAR
               fell from his eye.

And that is the story of how the Somerville Bulldogs went

from nothing to something and became...

Little League

Champions of Baseball

Did you just get chills?

I sure did!

183

Epilogue
(what does that even mean?!)

It's a fancy way to say "wrap it up". Kind of like an ending chapter, but not an "official" chapter.

No clue why — don't ask, we don't make the rules.

August 8

Ahhhh, Somerville...

Home of the Little League Baseball Champs!

There aren't many teams that go from a complete

shutout — losing record... to winning the championship.

BUT WE DID!!!!!!

Rumor in Somerville is that other athletic teams

have caught onto Coach Rod's NO PHONES rule and are

going use it too!! This means **one** cool thing — the BYK

JOURNAL is here to stay (how else will kids

communicate?!)

Until then, that's a wrap!

Bulldogs baseball season- OUT!

Dear kid reading this book,

Hey there rule breaker! Don't act like you don't
remember! You know... the whole 'DO NOT OPEN'
warning at the start of the journal... you totally
ignored it!

You weren't supposed to be here, reading any
of this. But HERE YOU ARE at the END of our
journal!

Thanks for breaking the rules and opening it
up. We hope you enjoyed!

Guess you are kinda part of the Bulldog fam
now. It only makes sense you add yourself to
the journal too! On the next page add your
info... you know... make it official and all.

From,
Kolt "The Bolt" Ryan
&

Quinn Reed #0

Nash Walker
#15

Brendan Banks
#34

Kolten Ryan #3 Jack James #28

Ace Werley

Jayden Bell #2

The
Somerville Bulldogs

Parker
Reeves
#12

Spence Bryan
#46

Henry
Koin #20

Coach
Rodriguez

Coach Q

Amir Youssef #82

NEWEST member
of the team

SOMERVILLE Bulldogs

Name:

About me:

-LIKES-   -disLIKES-

Let's play a game....
Fill in the blanks

Most likely to make it to the Majors _____

Life of the party _____

Most likely to get hit by a pitch _____

Best pitcher _____

Greatest prankster _____

COACH ROD

Most likely to break a bat in HALF _____

Most likely to hit a dinger _____

Most likely to snuggle his mom at night _____

Best Backyard Kid _____
        (wait- trick question, backyard kids ban together)

About the authors

Mothers, educators, and authors, Regina Oakes and Danielle Devine are the creators of the *Journal of The Backyard Kids* series. Motivated by the world of youth sports (and with five collective children of their own), Regina and Danielle created the series to capture the life of ordinary kids experiencing not so ordinary events. Giving children a voice, their books are told from the perspective of children as they navigate sports and the world around them.

Not to be confused with a basic sports book; the journal is riddled with adventures, pranks, life-long friendships, heart-felt lessons, and epic rivalries. Readers who join the backyard kid adventures cannot help but feel like they are part of the backyard team!

Regina, a special education teacher and Danielle, a university

professor and registered nurse, met as neighbors in 2013.

Little did they know at that time, aligned lifelong dreams would

lead to their collaboration of writing children's books. The

'Journal of The Backyard Kids - Baseball Edition', published

in April 2023 is the first book in their series.

Just a couple of backyard
moms — taking the moment in
where it all began...

...in a backyard.

Made in the USA
Middletown, DE
23 March 2023

27094378R00110